ALIA MUHAMMAD BAKER
Saving a Library from War

BY LINDSAY BACHER

Published by The Child's World®
1980 Lookout Drive • Mankato, MN 56003-1705
800-599-READ • www.childsworld.com

Acknowledgments
The Child's World®: Mary Berendes, Publishing Director
Red Line Editorial: Design, editorial direction, and production
Photographs ©: Atef Hassan/Reuters/Corbis, cover, 1, 4, 21; AP Images, 7; James
Vellacott/Reuters/Corbis, 8; Peter Turnley/The Denver Post/Corbis, 9; Anja
Niedringhaus/AP Images, 11, 12; David Guttenfelder/AP Images, 15; Saurabh Das/AP
Images, 16; Timothy A. Clary/Getty, 18

ISBN 9781634074711

LCCN 2015946300

Printed in the United States of America
Mankato, MN
December, 2015
PA02286

ABOUT THE AUTHOR

Lindsay Bacher has a bachelor's degree in English and religion from Hamline
University, and a master's of art and religion degree from Yale Divinity
School. She lives in Minneapolis with her husband and two dogs, Sam
and Maggie.

TABLE OF
CONTENTS

Chapter 1

THE WAR BEGINS

Alia Muhammad Baker surrounded herself with books. As the head librarian at Central Library in Basra, Iraq, Baker walked the rows and rows of books, smiling as she helped patrons. In 2003, the 50-year-old woman had worked as the chief librarian of Central Library for 14 years.

Central Library in Basra was a place for people to come together and discuss ideas. Baker brought all different types of people to the library. She said, "My office wasn't a room for **dignitaries**. . . . It was a room for gatherings."[1]

The library's rules did not allow people to check out books and bring them home. But Baker knew the power of a good book. She thought reading was incredibly important. Baker would let people borrow books from the library, even though it was against the rules. She explained that in the Koran, "the first thing God said to Muhammad was 'Read.'"[2] Like most Iraqis, Baker is Muslim. In Islam, the Koran is the word

WHERE IS BASRA?

Basra is a port city in the southern region of Iraq, on the Shatt Al-Arab River. It is the second-largest city in Iraq, after Baghdad. More than 90 percent of the people in Basra can read, making the Central Library an important place in the city. Even though many people can read, not everyone finishes school. Only 43 percent of people go to high school. Baker's job as chief librarian was rare in Basra, where only one in 10 women work outside the home.

of God, and Muhammad is God's **prophet**. Baker took God's message to Muhammad very seriously.

At the same time Baker worked at Central Library, Saddam Hussein was serving as president of Iraq. Other countries, including the United States, thought that Hussein was hiding weapons of mass destruction. These weapons are very dangerous and can cause serious damage. United States President George W. Bush, along with other world leaders, told Hussein to leave Iraq or face war. But Hussein didn't leave Iraq, and a group of countries declared war on Iraq in March 2003.

During the Iraq war, the Iraqi government decided to use Central Library for their offices. They put an antiaircraft gun on the roof for protection. This gun was supposed keep the library from being bombed. The Iraqi government thought it would make the invading troops look bad if they bombed a library. Baker knew that in other wars, libraries had been destroyed. Before the war started, she asked Basra's governor if the library books could be moved to a safer location. Without giving a reason, he said no. The books had to stay in the library.

On April 6, 2003, American and British troops invaded Basra. Most people in Basra stayed inside during the fighting. Fires blazed in and around the city. Smoke filled the air. Helicopters circled the sky. As she saw the smoke and heard the troops

▲ Saddam Hussein served as president of Iraq
from 1979 to 2003.

fighting, Baker worried about the library. She feared that the
books she was supposed to take care of would be damaged. She
knew she had to do something. So Baker began to sneak books
out of the library, just like she used to let patrons take home
books to read.

Chapter 2

BASRA INVASION

In Basra, American and British troops fought soldiers from the Iraqi government. Many of the people in Basra did not like President Hussein, but Iraqi troops defended the city. It was a scary time for the people who lived in Basra. The invading troops brought tanks and **artillery.** The city was filled with the thundering noise of gunshots. The rumbling of the army tanks shook the earth.

◄ **British troops prepared to enter the city of Basra in April 2003.**

As the invading troops came into Basra, they played messages on loudspeakers to the people who lived there. The messages told people in Basra that it was dangerous on the streets and to stay inside. The water and electricity in the city

▲ **Thousands of citizens fled Basra during the war to find safety, food, and water.**

were cut off. Basra's water treatment plant stopped working. The city's water was not being cleaned. The people in Basra were forced to drink out of rivers, which were very dirty. The Red Cross, an organization that provides disaster relief, worried about a **humanitarian crisis** developing in Iraq.

Though the fighting continued, Iraqi people began to leave their houses. Some people started **looting** in Basra. They stole food, supplies, money, and other things from businesses and houses all around the city. Some people were angry at Hussein and destroyed pictures of him. British troops used a tank to pull down a statue of Hussein in Basra. **Chaos** filled the whole city.

The same day the troops invaded Basra, Baker called the library. She wanted to know it was protected during the looting and chaos. Government workers were supposed to take care of it during the invasion. But Baker discovered the government workers had fled. The streets of Basra were filled with looters. There was no electricity or water. Everything was in an uproar. No one knew if the library would survive the night.

A young Iraqi boy carried clean water delivered by American ▶ and British troops.

Chapter 3

SAVING THE BOOKS

The next morning, on April 7, Baker went to the library. As she traveled there, she heard artillery fire in the city. When she arrived at the building, Baker was shocked. Looters had already stolen the library's tables, desks, and chairs. The carpet had been ripped off the floor and carried away. The looters took all of the library's lights. But the bookshelves were still full. The books were safe.

Baker had already brought stacks of books to her house, but she knew she had to save more. She couldn't do it alone. Baker visited Anis Muhammad, the owner of the restaurant next door to the library. She begged him to help. Finally, Muhammad agreed. He remembered and said, "What could I do? It is the whole history of Basra."[3] Together, they came up with a plan.

Baker and Muhammad started pulling books off the shelves. They filled their arms with books. They carried them over the 7-foot (2.1-m) wall that stood between the library and Muhammad's restaurant. He stored the books there until Baker could safely bring them to her house.

Baker and Muhammad needed lots of help. There were tens of thousands

IRAQ'S HISTORY DESTROYED

Many historical documents and artifacts were ruined during the Iraq War. While thousands were saved from Central Library, more were destroyed in other buildings across Iraq. It's estimated that nearly one million books and ten million documents have been destroyed, lost, or stolen in Iraq since 2003.

of books in Basra's Central Library. Baker was determined to save them all. Muhammad's brothers and restaurant employees helped. Neighbors and other store owners joined in, too.

People helped carry the books one by one out of the building and over the wall. Then they started using boxes. Baker ripped down the curtains from the windows. She used them to wrap up big stacks of books, more books than she could hold in her arms.

Hussein Muhammad al-Salem al-Zambqa owned a perfume store near the library and helped rescue the library's books, too. Zambqa said, "The people who carried the books, not all of them were educated. Some of them could not write or could not read, but they knew they were precious books."[4]

Baker, Muhammad, al-Zambqa, and their neighbors carried books over the wall for hours. Day turned into night. Night turned back into day. Still they were lifting books off the shelves and over the library wall. After two days of work, they ran out of time.

Most of the books they rescued were written in Arabic. A few were written in English. Some of the books were priceless **artifacts**. One of the most precious books was a biography of the Prophet Muhammad. It was written in approximately AD 1300.

Buildings all over Basra fell victim to looters and thieves, ▶ including the Sheraton Hotel in central Basra.

Baker saved **manuscripts** that were hundreds of years old about Arabic grammar and the art of telling time. Another priceless book saved was a Koran written in Spanish. In all, Baker, Muhammad, and their friends had saved 30,000 books.

THAT'S HOW MANY BOOKS?

What do 30,000 books look like? For comparison, 30,323 people can fit into Harvard Stadium at Harvard University. If you stacked 29,035 12-inch rulers end-to-end, they would be as tall as Mount Everest. Thirty thousand miles is one-tenth of the distance from the Earth to the Moon. Thirty thousand is a lot of books, but it's still small for a library. The Library of Congress in Washington, D.C. has more than 37 million books and materials.

◄ Thousands of precious books were also saved from the National Library in Baghdad, Iraq, during the war.

Chapter 4

BAKER THE HERO

Nine days later, Central Library was in flames. The library had caught fire and burned to the ground. Muhammad saw the fire from his restaurant next door. He tried to get the British troops to help, but they wouldn't put out the fire. Baker was **distraught**. They had run out of time to save all the books. There were more than 10,000 books still in the library. She said, "I imagined that those books, those history

◄ Burned papers covered the floor of Central Library after it was mysteriously set on fire.

and culture and philosophy books, were crying, 'Why, why, why?'"[5] No one knew how the mysterious fire started.

The next day, British troops came to Muhammad's restaurant. His whole back room was filled with library books. If the soldiers found them, the British would think Muhammad stole the books. But the troops left without discovering the books. Muhammad said, "They did not know that the whole of the library was in my restaurant."[6]

As Basra became safer, Baker moved the books from Muhammad's restaurant to her home. There were books

THE IRAQ WAR

The Iraq War began in March 2003 and ended in December 2011. Life in Iraq was hard during the war. Many Iraqis experienced violence. Services like electricity and water did not always work. In 2013, it was estimated that more than 500,000 Iraqis died during the Iraq War. Nearly 8,000 Americans died while fighting in the Iraq War or working for American companies in the war zone.

everywhere. They were in piles around her home. Some even were put inside an old refrigerator. Baker gave stacks of books to her friends and library employees for safekeeping.

Baker's neighbors thought her behavior was odd. They thought she was a looter, stealing books for herself. "People were looking at me saying, 'Why is this woman bringing books?'" Baker said. They thought, "'People are stealing much more valuable things than that.'"[7] But Baker knew she was preserving Iraq's history. She was just waiting for the day when she could put them back on the shelves of Central Library.

The Central Library in Basra was rebuilt a year later in 2004. The rescued books went back on the library shelves. The people of Basra could read them again. Baker was renamed chief librarian and reopened the library.

Life wasn't easy for Baker during the Iraq War. The library burned down. Her city was occupied by foreign troops. People lost electricity and clean water. But Baker was a hero. She rescued 30,000 books and preserved Iraqi history and culture. People around the world heard about what Baker did. She became famous for saving Basra's library collection. Through her courage and **determination**, Baker made sure the people of Basra would have books to read, even after a war.

Ten years after the Iraq War ended, Central Library is still a ▶ place for people who love books to come together.

GLOSSARY

artifacts (AHR-tuh-fakts): Artifacts are old objects, often of great value. Some of the books in the library were valuable artifacts.

artillery (ar-TIL-lery): Artillery is a group of large guns. When the British and American troops invaded Basra, they brought a large amount of artillery.

chaos (KAY-ohs): Chaos is a state of disorder. During the war, Basra was filled with chaos since there was fighting everywhere.

determination (dee-TERM-in-nay-shun): Determination means someone is committed to doing a specific thing. Baker's determination saved the books in Central Library.

dignitaries (DIG-na-tar-ees): Dignitaries are important people. Baker said that Central Library was a place for regular citizens, not for dignitaries.

distraught (dis-TROT): Someone who is very upset is distraught. Baker was distraught when the library burned down.

humanitarian crisis (hyoo-man-i-TER-ee-uhn CRY-sis): A humanitarian crisis happens if a large group of people don't have food, water, or other important services. The dirty water supply put Basra in a humanitarian crisis.

looting (LOOT-ing): Looting is when someone steals, usually during war. Some people were looting after the fighting ended during the war.

manuscripts (MAN-yoo-skripts): Manuscripts are old, handwritten documents. The library contained many old manuscripts.

prophet (PRAH-fit): A prophet is a religious leader who is believed to speak for God. Muslims believe Mohammed is God's prophet.

SOURCE NOTES

1. Shaila Dewan. "After the War: The Librarian; Books Spirited to Safety Before Iraq Library Fire." *New York Times*. The New York Times Company, 27 Jul. 2003. Web. 5 Apr. 2015.

2. Ibid.

3. Ibid.

4. Ibid.

5. Ibid.

6. Ibid.

7. Ibid.

TO LEARN MORE

Books

Ellis, Deborah. *Children of War: Voices of Iraqi Refugees*. Toronto: Groundwood Books, 2010.

Ruurs, Margriet. *My Librarian Is a Camel: How Books Are Brought to Children Around the World*. Honesdale, PA: Boyd Mills Press, 2005.

Stamaty, Mark Alan. *Alia's Mission: Saving the Books of Iraq*. Decorah, IA: Dragonfly Books, 2010.

Winter, Jeanette. *The Librarian of Basra: A True Story from Iraq*. Boston: Houghton Mifflin Harcourt, 2005.

Web Sites

Visit our Web site for links about Alia Muhammad Baker:
childsworld.com/links

Note to Parents, Teachers, and Librarians: We routinely verify our Web links to make sure they are safe and active sites. So encourage your readers to check them out!

INDEX